A Publication of the
**National Wildfire
Coordinating Group**

Wildfire Prevention

Conducting School Programs Guide

PMS 453

MARCH 1996

Wildfire Prevention

Conducting School
Programs
Guide

This publication is available online at http://www.nwcg.gov

NOTES

PREFACE

This Wildfire Prevention Guide is a project of the National Wildfire Coordinating Group. This is one in a series designed to provide information and guidance for personnel who have interests and/or responsibilities in fire prevention.

Each guide in the series addresses an individual component of a fire prevention program. In addition to providing insight and useful information, each guide suggests implementation strategies and examples for utilizing this information.

Each Wildfire Prevention Guide has been developed by Fire Prevention Specialists and subject-matter experts in the appropriate area. The goal of this series is to improve and enhance wildfire prevention programs and to facilitate the achievement of NWCG program goals.

The development group is made up of the following representatives:

Pat Durland, Project Leader, USDI, BLM/NIFC, Fire Prevention
Bill Clark, USDI, National Park Service, NIFC, Fire Prevention
Danny Jones, USDA, Forest Service, Sierra National Forest
Tara Johannsen, USDI, BLM, Prineville, Oregon
Steve Eckert, Assistant State FMO, Wyoming State Office, BLM
Dana Dierkes, National Park Service, Washington D. C.
Kathryn Hooper. Fire Prevention Officer, Las Vegas District, BLM
Gene Ottonello, FCO, Battle Mountain District, BLM
Pat Kidder, California State FMO, California State Office, BLM
Bruce Turbeville, California Department of Forestry and Fire Protection

NOTES

CONTENTS

1.1 INTRODUCTION

This Guide is one in a series of Wildfire Prevention Guides that are designed to be used as a tool to enhance the delivery of basic wildfire prevention and safety programs.

The information here provides guidance in presenting wildfire prevention and safety messages to audiences at the following educational levels: 1) Preschool; 2) Primary Grades (Kindergarten through Second Grade); 3) Intermediate Grades (Third through Sixth Grade); and 4) a basic introduction to presenting wildfire prevention messages to older students at the junior and senior high school levels.

This guide was developed by a group of subject matter experts experts who contributed their time, energy and knowledge to the task of providing this information for fire prevention personnel.

NOTES

1.2 UNDERSTANDING THE EDUCATIONAL SETTING

The first step in reaching out to students and presenting a fire prevention message is to know and understand the local school system and the educational setting .

Personal contact with school officials by agency personnel is an important part of any wildfire prevention program. To be effective, each contact must be planned carefully in advance and delivered formally or informally with enthusiasm. This is the chance to "sell" the wildfire prevention goals. Initial steps to take include the following:

- Contact school administrators.

- Seek approval from school officials to contact school administrators; use proper local policies.

- Be prepared to present an outline and supportive materials to school officials when applying for approval of the Wildfire Prevention Pro gram presentation.

- Make personal contacts with teachers.

- Make contacts through other means (e.g., Parent-Teacher Association)

1.3 THE TEACHERS INPUT

The presentation of a wildfire prevention program will be enhanced if input is obtained from the teacher during the planning process. This will show interest and professionalism as well as provide helpful information to improve the effectiveness of the presentation.

The following actions should be taken to maximize program effectiveness in the classroom:

- Speak with the teacher and try to get a feel for current understanding of fire and wildfire prevention by the students.

- Ask what fire safety issues have been presented in the past.

- Ask what objectives the presentation must meet for the class/teacher/school.

- Learn what the teacher's time constraints are and tailor the presentation to meet those constraints.

- Visit the school in advance to ensure the facilities and classroom layout are adequate for the presentation. If a visit is not possible in advance, ask for detailed information by phone or mail.

- Ask for the number of students and if there are any students with special needs (deaf, physically impaired, non-English speaking students, etc.)

- If audiovisual aids are to be used, BE SURE to ask about special needs such as room setup, power supply, screens, window shades, etc.

- A good rule of thumb for supervision is to have one adult for every 10 children. It is also a good idea to send information, guidelines and rules to the teacher or program leader in advance of the presentation.

1.4 GUIDELINES FOR KNOWING THE TARGET AUDIENCE AND TAILORING THE PRESENTATION

The information on the following pages provides a basic look at student development and will help to understand the learning capabilities of each grade level that will be contacted.

Additionally, this section suggests some presentation methods and techniques to assist the instructor in tailoring the presentation to the ability and skill of the students at each level.

Preschool

What you should know

Studies have shown that reaching children of preschool age with a fire prevention message is essential in our effort to reduce wildland fires. Effective wildfire prevention and fire safety education geared toward preschool children can substantially reduce the number of wildland fires.

Preschool children are just beginning to be more aware of what goes on around them and may have some mistaken concepts. Preschoolers test their concepts in many ways. Dramatic play and talk are ways of testing what they have seen and heard. Discussing their ideas with adults is one of the most effective ways in which preschoolers clarify their concepts. Firsthand experience is helpful and should be included when talking to preschoolers.

Methods of instruction

You can help these children develop correct concepts of fire prevention by using the following methods:

- **Give simple information.** Simple fire prevention materials should be used and thoroughly explained to the children. Complicated materials are not understood and should never be used.

- **Let them touch and see.** To increase the children's understanding of the message, include items that allow the children to use all of their senses.

- **Present information a little at a time.** Too much information at once is usually overwhelming and is not absorbed by a preschool child.

- **Answer all questions to the children's satisfaction.** If you're not sure you have done so, ask them. Some children will use this opportunity to tell a story and it is up to you to steer the presentation back to answering questions.

Presentation techniques

There are special techniques that can be used with preschool children. The instructor can become a part of the class and let the children feel at ease. The following tips can aid in the presentation and help the students become more receptive to the message:

- Sit on the floor with them or be at the same eye level.

- During the presentation, pass around items being talked about. This helps the children become actively involved, gives them something for a reference, and enhances their understanding of the message.

- Use visual aids wherever possible (use large, simple images).

- Move slowly; do not use rapid movements.

- Speak slowly in a quiet and calm voice.

- Introduce a few ideas as a time; be sure the children understand them.

- Remember that a workable-size group of preschoolers is between five and 20 students -- the fewer the better. Verify the number of students beforehand in order to better plan the program.

- Relate the information in the message to something within the children's experience (barbeque, fireplace, gas or wood stove, birthday candles, etc.)

Primary grades
(Kindergarten through second grade)

What you should know

Children in the primary grades (kindergarten through second grade) are usually active 5- to 7 -year-olds. They are alert, keen observers with vivid imaginations. They learn best by participating and being involved in activities with their hands, feet, and body.

The primary-grade child is a pretender and imitator who is easily influenced by the behavior of adults. The image that is portrayed can make a lasting impression on him or her.

Attention spans among age groups vary considerably. Plan the program length, class size and course content accordingly. Do not try to present too many ideas at one time. Use one or two simple themes.

Kindergarten and first-grade children require short, easy lessons no longer than 10 to 15 minutes in length. Second graders may accept an interesting, well-illustrated program of no longer than 25 minutes. Indoor programs should never go beyond one school period for any primary class.

The ideal group size is 20 to 30 children. This should be the rule for kindergarten and first grade. Sometimes, to accommodate tight school schedules, it may be necessary to combine classes. However, avoid mixing grade levels if possible.

The language used must be appropriate to the age level being taught. A 7-year-old second grader can grasp the meaning of some words that are foreign to the 5-year-old kindergarten student.

Observe the children when speaking. If they do not understand a concept, try using different words or relate an example in another way.

Presentation techniques

The techniques to use in reaching primary-grade students differ from those used with younger children. The following are some suggested techniques to use when presenting a program to students at this educational level:

- Identify with the group. For instance, put yourself in the place of the child and it can be observed that by hovering over them, you appear to be a large, overwhelming person. Get down to their level by sitting on the floor or a small chair. Meet them eye-to-eye.

- These are impressionable children who may hold on to every word and action, so be careful what is said or done.

- Use slow, deliberate movements.

- Speak clearly and distinctly.

- Repeat often, emphasizing and explaining important words.

- Look them in the eyes as you glance around the group.

- Answer each question completely and be sure the children understand the answer. Have the class help in answering.

After the presentation

After concluding the presentation to the class, provide materials to the teacher(s) to continue teaching the subject matter during the school year. Write a thank-you letter to the teacher as soon as possible, using the following suggestions:

- Word it so the teacher can read it to the class.

- Design it so that it serves as a review of the presentation.

Intermediate grades (Third through sixth grade)

What you should know

Intermediate-grade children have perhaps the greatest range in mental and physical growth than any other age group.

- Some third-grade and most fourth-grade students have begun the systematic study of grammar. They are learning to use telephones, write letters, and use dictionaries. Their vocabularies are increasing, and they have begun to calculate fractions and geometry.

- Ten-year-old fifth graders can be eager, receptive, happy scholars who are willing to accept any doctrine and who will be influenced by it in the future.

- Fifth graders are gaining control of their limbs, so they are less awkward. Their vocabulary is steadily increasing. They are starting to use graphs, decimals, geometric figures, and they solve problems in many ways. Their enthusiasm makes them uninhibited singers with generally good rhythm.

- Fifth-grade students have progressed rapidly in their scientific knowledge and development. They have expanded their understanding of the world far beyond their own area to regional and ethnic groups in the United States who contributed to the culture and wealth of our nation. They are learning the part individuals and government play in conserving natural resources.

- Fifth graders are beginning to comprehend science and can assimilate the fundamentals of ecology, land management and combustion. They now can relate watershed fires to loss of water and distinguish between renewable and nonrenewable resources.

- Eleven-year -old sixth graders are applying the basic skills developed in grades four and five. They are being introduced to global geography; relationships that exist among peoples of the world; and the basic facts of the physical world: land, water, air and the interdependence of natural resources.

Presentation techniques

Through the cooperation of principals and teachers, we can take advantage of the fifth-grade basic course of study to incorporate fire prevention and conservation into spelling, vocabulary, mathematics, science, social studies, and physical education.

Fifth-grade fire prevention programs can range from a simple display card to a presentation as formal as a locally sponsored Junior Fire Fighter Program. Or, if money, personnel and time allow, fire prevention programs can become as comprehensive as you want.

The sixth-grade program can be patterned almost entirely after the fifth grade, but it should be more detailed, taking advantage of increased maturity.

At each of these levels, students understand cause-and-effect relationships. Emphasize these relationships when presenting a message about fire prevention and the use, sharing and appreciation of public lands.

Junior high school

What you should know

The typical junior high school student is experiencing an awkward stage of adjustment and development. These youngsters are undergoing the mental and physical challenges of adolescence.

This age group is not only impressionable and creative but also inconsistent. Anyone teaching this age group must be alert and flexible to cope with its challenging behavior patterns. These youngsters are inclined to react spontaneously and somewhat unpredictably to changes in classroom situations. In spite of all this, these children are probably the most rewarding of all to instruct.

Seventh through ninth graders are interested in the things that affect them. Therefore, it is critical that natural resource and fire prevention education relate directly to the audience or to some other interest that is important to them. Responsibility and dollars do not get their attention.

Presentation techniques

Show how wildland resource losses from fires affect them. Make the presentation relate to their world and teenage interests. Describe fire prevention step-by-step with unfolding drama on their terms. Explain what fires can do to them and their future. Cite examples of recent local or regional fires they may have seen or heard about.

Increase the presentation effectiveness by meeting the students' needs. Ideally, any effort to extend fire prevention programs into junior high schools should be approached from a curriculum standpoint. In other words,relate the presentation to the specific class.

For example, if a teacher requests a program for a general science class, realize that these classes normally explain the principles of combustion but do not show how carelessness is at fault in many fires. The presentation should consist mostly of demonstrations about combustion principles; the fire triangle; Type A, B and C fires; or fire causes. Fire prevention messages can be introduced while the focus remains on the curriculum subject.

In a general science class, for example, the talk might be about the combustion that occurs when a cigarette is tossed into dry fuel and explain the factors leading to fire spread, the effects of topography, and so on. In a biology class, attention can be drawn to the life-science aspects of the forest or rangeland. For instance, relate the effects of fire to the balance of nature. In an English class, slogans or essay contests would be appropriate. For art classes, students can concentrate on signs, posters, paintings or models.

Junior high school groups are impressionable. Although they tend to resist authority and question traditional values, they readily accept the teaching of nonacademic professionals who make guest appearances in their classes.

The best teaching approach for junior high school students is to orient the presentation to the subject matter they are studying in that particular class. Involve the students by using material that is relevant to their experience level. The choice of technique (lecture, demonstration, movies, slides, student workshop or field trip) may vary, but the method selected must fit both the teaching situation and any classroom limitations.

High school program

What you should know

High schools offer an opportunity to reach young, active citizens with fire prevention messages. There is potential for both immediate and long range results. Most students are fairly serious and generally well-informed about the world around them. Even average or below-average students probably have been exposed to advanced teaching techniques and to a wider range of subjects than some adults.

Whenever possible, programs should be given to classes where students' interest and knowledge in a subject are similar. For example, a science class may be limited to pupils who have completed prescribed courses and have shown an interest in the subject matter. In such cases, a program could be designed to fit both the interest and knowledge of the students. Scientific aspects of fire prevention and fire-safe communities should be of interest and could be easily understood. Programs given to a student assembly where interests and abilities vary greatly would need to be much more general.

As with all presentations, the preparation should include learning about the audience beforehand. Talk to the teacher(s) or principal. They have an interest in the presentation being a positive learning experience, so they are glad to help by talking about the students' interests, educational level, etc.

Agency personnel have a definite advantage over regular teachers and most other guest instructors. Uniforms are admired and respected by most high school students. Caution must be exercised, however, to ensure technical accuracy. Alert high school students quickly detect errors, so instructors must be careful that they present correct information.

Most high school students have one thing in common: they are testing their sophistication. If they have any interest in a subject, they want to know "why?"

Any well-prepared and well-presented fire prevention program is acceptable for high school presentations, but programs combining visual aids with lectures have more impact than lectures without aids. Adequate results can be achieved with a straight lecture, but this technique should be used only when visual materials are not available or are not feasible.

1.5 HANDLING PROBLEMS AND PROBLEM STUDENTS

Preschool through second grade

Sometimes there may be little problems that plague you, but if you are well-prepared and make the presentation interesting, you can overcome the small difficulties and avoid major ones. Sometimes, no matter how much is done, a disruptive child may interrupt the presentation. Do not lose your composure or let things get out of hand. Make the problem child your helper. Let the child hand out materials, sit next to you, hold up displays, or draw on the blackboards. If necessary, seek the teacher's assistance in dealing with or removing a problem student.

Intermediate grades through high school

How do you appeal to the youngster who may be a problem? What do you do and say? How do you win over such a student? There is no set pattern because these students are individuals who do not always understand themselves. Approach them as young adults. Interject humor, and use demonstrations to keep them interested in you and the presentation.

Stimulate students' intellects with facts and concepts that are special or unique to our profession. Do not try to deceive students. They are perceptive and alert and can see through your efforts.

NOTES

1.6 DEVELOPING PRESENTATION SKILLS: GUIDELINES AND TECHNIQUES

This section provides information that lays the groundwork for improving instructor presentation skills. These guidelines are designed to help give professional and effective fire prevention presentations in school settings.

Thoroughly developed, effective presentations can increase student participation, understanding and support. Therefore, they need to be an integral part of fire prevention programs. Increasing knowledge and experience as a presenter leads to increased confidence and ability, which in turn leads to more informed, adaptable and effective presentations.

As a minimum, the following should be considered:

- Become familiar with the material, program and props well in advance of the presentation.

- Wear an agency uniform, when appropriate.

- Adjust the presentation to meet the educational and skill level of the audience.

- Practice presenting a professional agency image.

Preparation

Determine in advance what the talk is about and the type of presentation that is planned. Is the goal to inform, persuade, sell an idea or project, incite to action, entertain, or to present an award? After selecting the subject and the type of presentation, outline the points to cover.

- Find an interesting starting point or attention-grabber. In the opening, try to establish rapport with the audience. The more that is known about the audience beforehand, the easier this will be.

- Fill in the body of the talk with the points to cover, keeping in mind the background, interests and concerns of the audience.

- Select a good concluding point. Without a definite conclusion, the instructor might flounder helplessly and cause embarrassment.

- It is helpful to partially memorize the beginning and ending of your talk. Never memorize the body of your talk.

- Prepare psychologically. Much of the success of the talk depends on the instructor's frame of mind. Think positively about it and the talk will be easier to give. Look forward to the opportunity to present issues of prime concern to the audience.

Practice

Rehearse the talk. Carefully work out the elements of sequence, timing and continuity. Remember that more practice time is needed to develop a formal talk that sounds natural and is interesting and personal.

Have someone else listen to the practice talk to help smooth out rough areas. If visual aids are used, determine where to stand so the audience can see without obstructions. Slides, movies, and other visuals need to be run through for timing, sequence and appropriateness. If possible, rehearse in the actual presentation setting with the projectors, recorders, etc., that will be used during the actual presentation.

Experiencing nervousness and stage fright is normal for most people. Apprehension about the audience reaction is often a positive element, because, the very nature of this feeling can make the instructor more alert. While there is no single method to remove the nervousness and fears, thorough preparation and practice are likely the most effective tools to help deal with these feelings. The more prepared the instructors are, the more comfortable they will be before, during and after the presentation.

Presentation

When the time comes to perform, try to relax. If you are nervous, experts on public speaking suggest that you take a deep breath and exhale slowly. Before you are introduced, be sure your uniform is in order and then leave your attire alone. When you are introduced, rise, face the person who introduced you, pause a few seconds to let things settle down, and then make your opening statement.

Personality is one of the most important ingredients of your talk. You have the ability and prestige, or the group (or your supervisor) would not have asked you to speak. You arrived at your present position because of your talents and effort, coupled with knowledge and years of personal experience.

All of these together help make up your personality, which is the most effective tool you possess. A little humility and a smile will put your audience at ease and gain their support.

- **Good posture before an audience is a must.** Stand upright. Let your hands rest naturally at your sides or rest them on the lectern. Do not hold eyeglasses, pens or pencils, books, magazines, other objects, or jingle change in your pocket. Handling these objects is a nervous habit that tends to distract your audience from what you are saying.

- **Maintain good eye contact with your audience.** Visually scan the audience. Do not settle on one individual, the wall, ceiling, floor, or podium. If reading something, look up frequently to let your audience know you have not forgotten them.

- **Use gestures.** They add interest. Do not flail your arms, but use gestures pertinent to your remarks. Let your gestures be natural, not artificial.

- **Involve the audience with props whenever possible.** For example, simple, colorful and creative items that encompass the use of many senses are suggested, especially for young audiences.

If you sit down after speaking and realize that you left out parts of your talk that were very important, don't dwell on it or worry about it. Use it as a learning experience and decide that you will do better next time.

Most of the principles described here are accepted Toastmasters' practices and techniques. If you hold a job that involves frequent talks before groups, you should consider joining a speaker's club or enrolling in an adult education class in your community. You should practice public speaking whenever possible. You can learn something from each presentation, a each speech makes you more confident for the next one.

1.7 AUDIOVISUAL AIDS

Too often, people think that motion pictures and slides represent the entire scope of visual aids. This is not so. Charts, graphs, pictures, models, and sketches are classified as visual aids. Visual aids have unlimited possibilities; their use is limited only by the resourcefulness of the people who use them.

Use audiovisual aids whenever possible because they convey information, knowledge, and ideas in the shortest possible time. Such aids, however, must be appropriate for the age and educational level of the audience. While audiovisual tools are an important element in presentations to young audiences, the audiovisual aids discussed on the following pages are targeted primarily for older students and adult audiences.

Verbal explanations supplemented by visual aids attract attention and create interest more rapidly than verbal explanations alone. Use a combination of visual aids if the situation permits. The major part of what people hear is forgotten in a relatively short time. On the other hand, things people see <u>and</u> hear make a more lasting impression and increase retention.

Many things cannot be taught, explained or sold without the aid of demonstrations, models, charts, diagrams or pictures. Visual aids can be the difference between confusion and understanding.

When deciding what type of visual aids to use in the presentation, consider the following:

- **The objective.** What is expected of the audience as the result of the program? Only after this has been decided can the objective be prepared to consider the best method of visualization to use.

- **The audience.** What age and educational level is the audience? What type and complexity of audiovisual aids will get and keep their attention? What audiovisual aids will best impart the message and increase retention of what the audience learns?

- **The size of the audience.** This determines the size of charts and lettering. A small group sitting in front of the instructor does not require large charts and lettering. However, everything must be large enough for the entire audience to see.

- **Location of the audience.** If the program is presented in various locations, films, video tapes or slides are best because they can be shown in either close quarters or large auditoriums. They also are relatively easy to transport and handle.

- **Size of the budget.** This question must be answered before determining the types of visual aids to use.

- **Keep it simple.** A cardinal principle, simplicity, underlies the preparation of good visual aids. Each aid should deal with one central idea. The material should be rigorously edited to ensure that all nonessentials have been omitted. The remaining material should not be overcrowded. It is better to have two simple illustrations than one that is "busy" or complex.

When the material is presented, consider the following points:

- Do not let the audience see the visual aids until they are discussed, then cover or remove them when finished.

- Never read graphic displays to the audience. Any viewer can do this. Point out the significance of the material.

  After the presentation, evaluate the success of the material from the points of view of both the speaker and audience. If necessary, modify the material before it is used again.

Slide presentations

Automatic cameras with electric light meters, projectors with remote control features, lapse dissolve units and other electronic devices can improve the speaker's delivery and the audience's interest.

An effective slide presentation cannot be done without proper preparation. Using visuals requires more practice and finesse than the average speech by itself.

Each slide should be selected for its ability to make a point, attract attention, or imply a conclusion. Each slide should be the best available in composition and exposure. A perfect photograph with no apparent point, however, is of less value than a poorer shot with a definite message. In most cases, no photograph at all is better than a poor one.

How many slides should be used?

This is difficult to determine, especially for the beginner. There is no general rule of thumb. Each presentation must be considered separately. In a 30-minute presentation, as few as 12 or as many as 80 slides can be used successfully, depending on how they are used and what needs to be to shown. Generally, the fewer slides used, the more important it is for each one to be clear and convey the information you want to share.

Slides occasionally can be used in a series and projected very quickly for emphasis. There is no end to the possible uses if proper and conscientious thought is given to preparation.

Use note cards.

Note or index cards are very useful for preparing the written portion of the talk. They should be numbered to correspond with the slides as they are shown. Any changes or substitutions can be numbered and slipped into correct order without disturbing or retyping several pages of written material.

If standard 8" x 11" paper is used as a script, a good method is to divide the sheet in half vertically, mark one half audio, and the other half video, and then write the written presentation across from the visual that will be shown during that portion of the talk. Remember to leave plenty of space for easier reading.

Keep slides clean.

Most slides collect dust or fingerprints after being handled. Fingerprints can be removed by using a commercial liquid preparation. A camel-hair brush works well on dust.

Label and number slides.

Each slide should be labeled and numbered in case you drop or scramble them accidently. It does happen!!

Use good equipment.

A slide program is worthless without proper equipment.

- The projector should be checked before each use. Make sure that you have a spare bulb, a three-to-two prong adapter, at least one 15-foot or longer extension cord and a remote control extension.

  The lens should be clean, so have a static brush. Have a stand for the projector, in case it is needed. If a cartridge projector is used, correctly place and check each slide before arriving for the performance.

- Consider screen size and the focal length required for the lens. The screen should be filled by the picture, if possible. If you use both horizontal and vertical slides are used, have a square screen. If the screen is rectangular, either the vertical or horizontal slides are too large.

A few "don'ts" for speakers using slides:

- Don't apologize for any equipment or slides. If they are that poor, do not use them.

- Don't refer to a slide as a slide or picture. For example: "This slide shows ..." or "This is ..." or "This picture was taken ..." The audience knows that it is a picture and that they are watching the screen. Put your message across without these references.

- Don't wait until the last minute to arrive and assemble your equipment. It should be done before the crowd arrives. This gives the impression of organization, interest, professionalism and efficiency.

- Don't use slides showing information that is not in the script.

- Don't use slides that are irrelevant to the talk or that are poor examples of the point being discussed.

- Don't use slides containing poor photography caused by overexposure or poor composition.

- Don't use slides that lack continuity. This results when there is neither a connection between slides nor a smooth sequence of thought from one slide to the next.

DO let the audience know if you want them to ask questions during the performance or if there will be a question period after the presentation.

Using charts

Charts are inexpensive, easy to make and use, and easily changed or replaced. They can be very effective and flexible.

Charts help to win and hold the attention and interest of the audience. They can clarity ideas that would be difficult to express in words alone. An average speaker can excel in getting points across by using a well- organized set of charts.

The American Standards Association has set the following specific minimum criteria and size standards applicable to all types of displays and wall charts.

- Minimum size of the smallest lettering should be about 1/50 of the height of the sign.

- The standard shape of the chart or display is a height-to-width ratio of 3:4.

- A general rule also can be applied to determine the needed size of direct display charts. The minimum desired width must be 11 6 of the maximum viewing distance. For example, if a student at the rear of a classroom is 24 feet away from the front blackboard where a poster is displayed, the width of the poster must be at least four feet (1/6 of 24). Then the standard vertical height would be three feet (3:4 ratio).

The American Standards Association has also defined specific criteria for the size of lines and lettering used on charts. Refer to these criteria, if available. A good rule of thumb, however, is to make lines and letters large enough to be seen and read by <u>all</u> members of the audience, including those seated at the rear of the room.

Several factors must be considered when making charts. Review the material to be presented and become familiar with its major points and implications. The organization of the chart may vary according to the particular purposes.

- If the chart contains an overview given early in a presentation, it may show several different points briefly.

- If the chart contains a summary, the information should be quite specific.

- If more than one chart is needed to cover the topic, prepare separate charts and select a good sequence. Two chart forms are used to present data in sequence: the strip chart and the flip chart.

Types of charts

The strip chart is a single chart that contains various steps covered with strips of paper. Important points may be exposed individually by removing each paper strip as desired. Strips can be attached to the chart with masking or cellophane tape.

The flip chart is a series of charts prepared in sequence that are bound together at the top. As the instructor completes the discussion, each chart is pulled up over the easel to expose the next chart. Flip charts can be bought ready made or prepared from several sheets of newsprint or large drawing paper. Fasten the sheets together at the top with thin metal or wood strips on the front and back. Mount the supporting strip at the top of an easel.

Good charts often use a mixture of pictures, drawings, cartoons, graphs, diagrams, and words.

Using a chalkboard

The chalkboard is probably the most familiar teaching device. A chalkboard is generally available, and it is one of the most widely used visual tools in any programmed talk. In spite of its availability, however, it is rarely used for graphic or pictorial presentations.

Sketching before a group holds the attention of the audience. For example, when a speaker turns to the board, selects a piece of chalk, and begins to draw, the movement attracts attention. During a "sleepy" period, if the speaker takes a piece of chalk and starts to sketch, the attention of each member of the audience is drawn to the board.

A carefully prepared chalkboard drawing made beforehand does not have the same vitalizing effect as a strong spontaneous sketch which emphasizes action or a key point made at the right moment during a program. The following are some points to follow when using a chalkboard:

- Do not hide the writing by standing directly in front of it. Write legibly and make sure everyone can see and read your writing.

- Do not write too much at one time. Speak to the group, then write a little, then stand aside and talk. Continue this procedure.

- Speak directly to the group; do not talk to the board.

These principles of using a chalkboard also apply to the use of easels and paper pads and the porcelain-surface boards.

Porcelain-surface boards

One of the latest developments in chalkboards is the porcelain-surface board. Because of its steel base, magnets adhere to its face and papers can be displayed without tacking, taping or defacing the board surface.

Instructional materials equipped with magnetic holders are available in many colors. Magnetic frame sticks can hold charts to the steel surface, or magnetic pointers or arrows can be used to highlight the item being discussed.

The magnetic board is particularly useful when displayed items are moved as problems change or solutions are developed.

Easels and paper pads

Another "chalkboard" is a portable easel that holds king-sized paper sheets. The big advantage of this device over the conventional blackboard is that conference notes, sketches or ideas can be saved for future reference.

The lines on paper pads are usually light blue and barely visible from a short distance. Pads can be purchased unlined or in 1/2-inch or 1-inch squares. The lines can help in making your the charts or draw diagrams before groups.(also see flip charts on page 28)

1.8 HANDLING UNSOLICITED AND UNPLANNED REQUESTS

Occasionally unexpected requests will be received to present a fire prevention program. These requests may put the instructor in the awkward position of wanting to add the presentation to the schedule but being short on time, materials and promotional items.

While it is difficult to always avoid such predicaments, you can significantly reduce their impact by doing the following:

- Carefully consider the request to see if it meets the fire prevention program goals.

- Determine if it is worth the time it will require to gather extra materials and promotional items and organize a presentation.

- If the schedule won't allow you to meet the request, try to provide a Teachers' Guide, if available, including lesson plans so the teacher can present the material. Include names arid phone numbers as a reference in case the teacher has any questions.

- Try to utilize existing programs to meet the needs of the unplanned requests.

- Consider asking other presenters from within the agency or cooperative agency to fulfill the request.

- On an annual basis, budget for and order additional items to help cover unplanned requests. Also, know how to obtain more materials when necessary.

NOTES

PART 2

Wildfire Prevention Program

Sample Lesson Plan - Good Fire, Bad Fire

Sample Lesson Plan- Good Fire is Helpful

Suggestions for a Fire Prevention Program
Script Narrative and Props

Educational Props and Teaching Aids

Evaluating Your Wildfire Prevention Program

NOTES

2.1 SAMPLE LESSON PLAN
GOOD FIRE, BAD FIRE

Title: Good Fires and Bad Fires

Grade Level: Preschool to Second Grade

**Time
Required:**   20 Minutes

Skills: The student, by participating in this activity, will
                      be able to distinguish between good and bad fires.

**Learning
Objectives:**   The students will be able to correctly identify good
                      fires and bad fires. In addition, the children will be
                      able to complete an activity sheet by connecting
                      the Good Fire or Bad Fire examples with a Happy
                      Flame or Angry Flame character. The activity
                      sheets will be available in the teacher packets.

Materials: Good Fire - Bad Fire activity sheets.
                      Note: This activity asks the student to draw a line
                      from the Happy Flame to the Good Fires and to
                      draw a line from the Angry Flame to the Bad Fires.

                      Good Fire - Bad Fire Flash Cards:

                      #1   Meet the Wildfire Prevention Team

                      #2   Meet the Good Fire and Bad Fire characters

                      #3   Barbeque

#4   Child with clothes burning

#5   Wildfire

#6   Campfire

#7   Fireplace

#8   Kids playing with matches

#9   Birthday candles

#10   House fire

Procedures: You will be telling the children that we will be discussing fire safety and learning how they can be safe from fire. We will ask the children what fire is. The desired response is that it is hot and that it burns. If they do not respond this way, then we will lead them to this conclusion. We will emphasize to them that fire is dangerous and something that adults must use and supervise.

We will then let the children discuss whether or not all fire is bad. We will tell them that there are good fires and bad fires. It is important to remind them that fire is dangerous, it CAN hurt them and they should NEVER play with fire.

Not all fire is bad. We will ask them to give an example of a Good Fire. We will also give them a few examples to introduce the concept of Good Fire; i.e., fireplace, birthday candles or campfire.

Similarly, we will give them some examples of Bad Fire and discuss the differences with them, letting them make the distinction between good and bad fire. It will be stressed that whether a fire is good or bad, it is dangerous and must be used only by adults.

2.2 SAMPLE LESSON PLAN FOR GOOD FIRE IS HELPFUL

Title:	Good Fire is Helpful
Grade Level:	Kindergarten through 5th Grade
Time Required:	20 minutes (or more if discussion and time allow)
Skill:	Students will use their knowledge of helpful and harmful fires to solve problems related to keeping fires helpful and not allowing them to become out-of-control wildfires.
Learning Objectives:	Students will understand the concepts of useful and helpful fires as well as harmful fires. Students will also understand aspects of fire safety.
Materials:	• Narrative script (on the following pages).
	• Props (or slides, if available) to emphasize the appropriate topic.
Procedures:	We will be telling the children that we will be discussing fire safety and learning how they can be safe from fire. We will ask the children what fire is. The desired response is that it is hot and that it burns. If they do not respond this way, then we will lead them to this conclusion.

We will emphasize to them that fire is DANGEROUS and something that adults must use and supervise.

We will then let the children discuss whether or not all fire is bad. We will tell them that there are Good Fires and Bad Fires. It is important to remind them that fire is dangerous, it CAN hurt them and they should NEVER play with fire.

Not all fire is bad. We will ask them to give an example of a Good Fire. We will also give them a few examples to introduce the concept of good fire, e.g. fireplace, birthday candles or campfire.

Similarly, we will give them some examples of Bad Fire and discuss the differences with them, letting them make the distinction between good and bad fire. Fire safety will be stressed as will the concept that whether a fire is good or bad, <u>ALL</u> fire is dangerous and must only be used or supervised by adults.

2.3 SUGGESTIONS FOR A FIRE PREVENTION PROGRAM SCRIPT AND PROPS

The following script and prop suggestions provide a framework which can be adapted, built upon, expanded and tailored to specific geographic areas, audiences and fire prevention program needs. Props may be slides, pictures or other visual depictions.

1. *Prop or slide showing parent burning leaves or a ditchbank*

Question:

What does parent need to know about and have on hand when using fire?

Answer:

Burning Permit if required by local law.

Weather. Strong winds may cause fire to spread and grow.

Shovel. Always have a shovel nearby in case fire starts to burn beyond planned boundaries.

Garden Hose. Always have water near to help cool fire if it starts to spread.

Never burn near buildings such as garages, sheds or other structures that could catch on fire.

Question:

What are good and bad aspects of these fires?

Answer:

Good - gets rid of dead leaves and weeds. Also the ashes can be used to help gardens and flowers grow.

Bad - none, as long as fire doesn't get big, out of control or the smoke bothers others.

2. *Prop showing campfire near tents in a camping area*

Question:

What precautions should be or have been taken to safely use the campfire?

Answer:

The campfire area should be cleared of grass, twigs and branches.

Keep it small. Fires should be contained in a pit about two feet by two feet in size and the pit should be lined with rocks and bare dirt (or concrete in some developed campsites).

Keep it away from tents. Fires should never be built near tents or other things that can catch on fire. Remember, sparks may fly out of the fire and travel several feet.

Have a shovel and water handy. Always keep some water and a shovel nearby so that if the fire does start to escape from the fire pit, you can put it out.

Never leave a campfire unattended. If someone isn't there to watch the fire, it could escape its limits. If you are going to bed or you are going off to fish, hike or play, always be sure the fire is dead out.

Even when there are just coals in the fire, put water on it and stir it up with the shovel before leaving.

Don 't build a fire on a windy day. Strong wind gusts can blow sparks and fire outside of the fire pit.

Question:

What are the good and bad aspects of a campfire?

Answer:

Good - They keep us warm in the outdoors.

They can dry both wet clothes and us.

They are fun for roasting marshmallows and hotdogs and other cooking.

Bad - none... as long as it is kept small and under control.

3. *Prop showing vegetation close to a house or structure*

Tell students that in case of a wild or uncontrolled fire, this house or structure would be threatened and may burn.

Question:

What could this homeowner or property owner do to protect the house or structure? What could students do if this was their house?

Answer:

Make sure all weeds and flammable bushes are cleared away from the house or structure, ideally for at least 30 feet.

Plant only fire-resistant plants and shrubs near houses or other structures.

Don't stack firewood next to a house, garage or other structure. Wildfire can ignite the wood and then the house or other structure.

Trim tree branches so they don't hang over or next to the house or structure.

Don't put cedar (wooden) shakes on your house near wildlands unless the shakes are fire-resistant. If the house already has a wood roof, spray it with a fire-resistant solution.

Point out to students that it may be nice to live next to range or forest lands but it's very important to protect your home from fire.

4. *Prop(s) showing fireworks going off, such as a Roman candle or sparkler and large overhead fireworks. (You may want to bring some actual illegal fireworks that have been confiscated by law enforcement officials. Contact local police or fire departments or agency law enforcement personnel).*

Tell students that fireworks are fun and exciting but they must be used carefully so they don't start a wildfire.

Question:

What can we do to be sure fireworks don't start fires?

Answer:

Always have an adult present. Fireworks are dangerous and should only be lit by an adult. Fireworks can burn you.

Don't use fireworks near grass land or forests. Fireworks can get out of control and ignite a fire very easily in dry grass or brush. In the forest they can start fires in pine needles on the ground and burn tall trees.

Always have some water and a shovel nearby when you use fireworks, just in case one misfires or starts a fire.

Stress that fireworks of any type *are not allowed* on public lands!

5. *Prop(s) showing people outdoors (hunters, bikers, or people having a picnic) doing foolish things (littering, throwing a burning cigarette, etc.).*

Ask the students if they see these people doing anything they shouldn't be doing and have them tell you why. Help them with some of the following ideas:

Carelessly tossed cigarettes can ignite a wildfire. Always be sure adults use the ashtray. If they smoke outdoors, make sure they do so only in an area cleared to bare dirt and that they crush out the cigarettes cold when they are finished.

Littering ruins a pretty view for others and it's a fire hazard because papers can ignite easily. Broken glass can work like a magnifying glass in the sun and ignite a fire.

Point out to the students that it's fun to enjoy the outdoors but we need to take care of it and leave it clean. Always clean up after yourself. It's always good to pick up litter even if it isn't yours.

6. *Slide(s) showing motorcycle riders and off-road-vehicle drivers in areas of grass and brush or in the forest.*

Tell students that some people's recreation includes riding motorcycles or off-road vehicles in the wildlands but they need to be careful so they don't start a fire. Ask the students if they know why/how people in the slide are risking starting a fire.

You may need to prompt the students with this one and explain that sparks from mufflers can ignite a fire in grass or pine needles.

Question:

How can these people be safe about riding in these areas?

Answer:

Be sure they have spark arresters in their mufflers.

Always stay on designated trails and don't wander off into the grass and brush or off the trails in the forest. (You can also incorporate an erosion message here.)

Note: Posters, photographs or other pictures may be obtained from a motorcycle or off-road-vehicle dealer in your area.

These are just a few suggestions for props and prevention messages. You may want to adapt them to your geographical area and specific audiences and incorporate them into your own prevention program.

2.4 EDUCATIONAL PROPS & TEACHING AIDS

ITEM GRADES:	P	K	1	2	3	4	5	6
SUPPORT MATERIALS:								
CLIP ART	X	X	X	X	X	X	X	X
STENCILS			X	X	X	X		
CALENDARS			X	X	X	X		
CLASS DECORATIONS	X	X	X	X	X	X	X	X
BANNERS	X	X	X	X	X	X	X	X
CREATIVE BOOKS			X	X	X	X		
CERTIFICATES/AWARDS	X	X	X	X	X	X	X	X
RUBBER STAMPS	X	X	X	X	X	X		
PENNANTS		X	X	X	X			
BULLETIN BOARD AIDS	X	X	X	X	X	X	X	X
STICKERS	X	X	X	X	X	X		
NAMEPLATES/TAGS	X	X	X	X	X			
MAGNETS	X	X	X	X	X			
BOOKMARKS					X	X	X	X
BOOKCOVERS					X	X	X	X
POSTERS	X	X	X	X	X	X	X	X
NOTEPADS PENCILS					X	X	X	X
CRAYONS	X	X	X	X	X	X	X	X
CHARACTER REPLICAS	X	X	X	X	X			
CHARACTER CUTOUTS	X	X	X	X	X			
BUTTONS	X	X	X	X	X			
TRADING CARDS			X	X	X	X	X	X
ACTIVITIES:								
PUZZLE-TABLE				X	X	X	X	X
PUZZLE-FLOOR	X	X	X	X	X			
SCHOOL PLAYS	X	X	X	X	X	X	X	X
SKITS	X	X	X	X	X	X	X	X

ITEM GRADES:	P	K	1	2	3	4	5	6
GAMES:								
BOARD	X	X	X	X	X	X	X	X
BINGO		X	X	X	X	X	X	X
MEMORY MATCH		X	X	X	X	X	X	X
ZIP CARD GAME					X	X	X	X
WORD GAMES		X	X	X	X	X	X	X
TWENTY QUESTIONS				X	X	X	X	
JEOPARDY TYPE					X	X	X	X
FLASHCARDS	X	X	X	X	X	X	X	X
LEARNING SHEETS	X	X	X	X	X	X	X	X
COSTUMES	X	X	X	X	X			
TELL-A-STORY	X	X	X	X				
DELIVERY TECHNIQUES:								
OVERHEAD TRANSPARENCY					X	X	X	X
SLIDE PROGRAMS	X	X	X	X	X	X	X	X
VIDEOTAPES	X	X	X	X	X	X	X	X
AUDIOTAPES	X	X	X	X	X	X	X	X
THEMATIC TEACHING		X	X	X	X	X	X	X
BIG BOOKS	X	X	X	X	X			
STORY CARDS	X	X	X	X	X			
PUPPETS	X	X	X	X	X			
PUPPET SHOWS	X	X	X	X	X			
MITT BOARD	X	X	X	X	X			
INTERNET			X	X	X	X	X	X
COMPUTER GAMES		X	X	X	X	X	X	X

2.5 EVALUATING YOUR WILDFIRE PREVENTION PROGRAM

As with all presentations, the school programs for wildfire prevention education are dynamic and always have room for change and improvement. A written evaluation provided by your audience is a valuable tool for measuring the effectiveness of your program and identifying strengths and weaknesses.

The Wildfire Prevention Program Evaluation form on the following page is one example of a written evaluation. It can be used as is, adapted to a specific audience, and requested from the teacher or students or both. The feedback you receive through this form can be referred to and used as you further develop and Improve your program.

Because of busy schedules and time constraints, some teachers may prefer to complete the evaluation and return it to you before you leave the classroom. Others may want to take more time or have a follow-up discussion with their students before responding. however, if the evaluation form is to be returned at a later date, ask that it be sent within a specified time, such as five days. This helps ensure that the information is fresh and the form won't be delayed indefinitely. Also, if you ask that the form be mailed back to you, attach a self-addressed, stamped envelope.

NOTES

WILDFIRE PREVENTION
PROGRAM EVALUATION

We would appreciate it if you would take a few moments to fill out this evaluation sheet and return it within five days to: {Name, Agency and Address} Thank You.

Question	Response		Comments
1. What is the age and grade level of your students?	Age Grade		
2. Is the lesson appropriate and/or effective for this age and grade level?	Yes	No	
3. How many students are in your group?			
4. Do you feel that your students understand the concepts that were presented?	Yes	No	
5. Was the lesson plan delivered in a manner that was easy for your students to understand?	Yes	No	
6. What was YOUR response to the program? Please score using a scale of 1 to 5 where 1 = poor and 5 = excellent.	Score		
7. What was your students' response to the program?	Score		
8. Would you be interested in having our agency visit your school again?	Yes	No	

Continued Next Page

9. Name of your preschool or school:

10. Address of your school:	Street:	
	City	Zip
11. Your name:	
12. School phone number:	( )

We are looking forward to the response about our program from you and your students. We value your opinion, and your comments will help us to continue improving our wildfire prevention program. Please return this form within the next five days.
Thank you for participating in this evaluation. We appreciate it!

Your comments on the overall program will be appreciated.
(Use additional sheets of paper if needed)